INTERVIEWING SKILLS

TIM

D1304426

FENN PUBLISHING COMPANY LTD

A DK PUBLISHING BOOK

Project Editor Sasha Heseltine
Editor Marian Broderick
US Editor Ray Rogers
Designers Elaine C. Monaghan,
Austin Barlow
Assistant Editor Felicity Crowe
Assistant Designer Laura Watson

DTP Designer Jason Little
Production Controller Alison Jones

Series Editor Jane Simmonds
Series Art Editor Jayne Jones

Managing Editor Stephanie Jackson
Managing Art Editor Nigel Duffield

First published in Canada in 1998 by
Fenn Publishing Company Ltd.,
34 Nixon Road, Bolton,
Ontario L7E 1W2

Visit us on the World Wide Web at
www.hbfenn.com

Copyright © 1998
Dorling Kindersley Limited, London
Text copyright © 1998 Tim Hindle

A record of Cataloging-in-Publication Data
is available from the National Library, Canada

ISBN 1-55168-178-1

Reproduced by Colourscan, Singapore
Printed and bound in Italy by Graphicom srl

CONTENTS

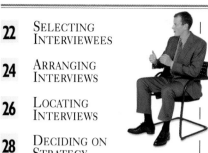

CONDUCTING AN INTERVIEW

ANALYZING AN INTERVIEW

INTRODUCTION

Whether it is a prominent part of your job or an isolated task, interviewing candidates to fill a position can be a complex and time-consuming process that requires careful consideration and planning. Interviewing Skills will help you devise a strategy that eliminates many of the problems involved in recruiting the best candidate every time. Practical advice helps you put the strategy into action, giving you the confidence and skills to succeed in your initial preparation, the job interview itself, and the follow-up procedure afterward. This book provides further invaluable help in the form of 101 concise tips, which are scattered throughout, and a self-assessment exercise allowing you to chart and evaluate your improvement with each interview you hold. Use this vital information again and again as your interviewing skills develop.

PREPARING FOR AN INTERVIEW

A job interview rarely lasts longer than an hour, but its consequences may last for years. In order to identify the most suitable candidate for a vacancy, prepare well in advance.

IDENTIFYING OBJECTIVES

An interview is a formal method of exchanging information between people. The interviewer needs to be clear about the purpose of the exchange to ensure that the time is used to give and obtain information that is relevant and revealing.

> **1** Evaluate every vacancy before calling for interviews.

> **2** Look for new blood rather than "one of us."

> **3** Imagine the ideal candidate for a vacant job.

DEFINING THE PURPOSE

The recruitment of new employees is one of the most important tasks a manager will undertake. Meeting candidates face to face provides the best opportunity for gathering information about their skills and experience and, ultimately, matching the right person to the job and to the organization.

In preparing for interviews, remember that your purpose is not only to evaluate the candidates, but also to describe the job accurately so that they can assess whether it is the right one for them. You will also need to represent your organization in the best light possible to attract good-quality candidates.

ASSESSING A VACANCY

Before any employer can set out to find a suitable candidate for a job, it is important that they establish the skills and experience the job requires.

Start by referring to the existing job description. Consider whether the job has changed over time, with the introduction of new technology, for instance. Does it now require different skills? Ask questions about the previous employee to decide if there is anything new that can be brought to the job. Were they suited to the job? Is a similar mix of abilities required in a new employee?

> **4** Review all job descriptions for your team when a vacancy is created.

ASSESSING JOB RELATIONSHIPS

An interviewer needs to assess how a job will relate to the roles of other employees. Where does it fit into the organizational hierarchy, and what will the role of the new job be within the existing team or department? To whom will the new employee report, and who will report to the new employee?

Bear in mind that there is usually room for some flexibility within an organizational structure. Consider, for instance, whether using new technology would allow a more junior employee to take on the responsibilities of a job previously done by a senior employee

▼ **GATHERING INFORMATION**
Discuss the requirements of a job with the present jobholder and those who work in the same team or department. This may lead to a reallocation of responsibilities among all roles and a reappraisal of the skills needed in a new employee.

INTERVIEWER
The interviewer obtains valuable information about the job from all those who work closely with the jobholder.

PRESENT JOBHOLDER   **SUBORDINATE**   **COLLEAGUE**   **SUPERIOR**

EVALUATING A ROLE

A new vacancy provides you with an opportunity to look closely at a job to evaluate its role within the company. Set aside time to identify specific changes that can be made to improve the job's value to the organization.

Start with the aims of the company. Have there been any directional changes in its goals, and has the job adapted to meet them? Ask other departments what their expectations of the job have been and whether these have been fulfilled.

Consider the assumptions you have about the knowledge and skills you think the job needs. Can you introduce useful new knowledge or skills into the company through the new appointment? Think also about the communication skills that are needed to make the job effective: are closer relationships with clients or other departments needed?

5 Use a vacancy as as an opportunity to reassess the reason for a job.

6 Check whether the qualifications required for a job have changed.

POINTS TO REMEMBER

- Not all vacancies need to be filled.
- Changes in business occur so rapidly that the need for a job may exist only for a short time.
- The best source of information about a job may be the previous jobholder.
- A vacancy can be an opportunity to redefine the responsibilities of a job.
- Currently unfulfilled tasks and duties can be added to a job description.
- It may be possible to reallocate work among current employees.
- Sometimes two people sharing a job can be more productive than one.

▼ REDEFINING A ROLE

This case looks at the way in which the role of librarian has been affected by information technology. Although the role was performed competently by the previous jobholder, a new applicant with updated skills shows how the scope of the job can be extended and improved to the benefit of the organization.

CASE STUDY

For 30 years, Great Universal Technology's library had been presided over by Thelma. In recent years, however, Thelma had become unhappy with the way her profession had changed. Although a proficient typist, she had never become comfortable with the computer, nor to the accelerating pace of corporate life. She decided it was time to retire.

Kevin, an ambitious young employee in the computer maintenance department, made an application for Thelma's job, arguing that the company needed a computer-literate "knowledge manager" – not a librarian. The company needed to be able to access the Internet as well as its own bookshelves. It also needed to bring together information from different departments of the company and to make it accessible to all staff. The chairman, impressed by Kevin's argument, gave him the job.

CONSIDERING CONDITIONS

When a job is vacated, consider whether you need to fill the job in the same way. If part of a job has become obsolete, due to changes in structure, for instance, consider appointing a part-time replacement. Use a jobsharing plan if the role needs different skills or to retain an employee who wants to work part time. If the work occurs only at certain periods, use freelancers or contract workers. Look at your finances: can one expensive employee be replaced by two junior employees, or vice versa?

> **7** When appropriate, offer flexible working hours.

CREATING A JOBSHARE ▶
Jobsharers who work during different times of the week need to establish a regular handover meeting. Dividing clients or customers between two employees can also create a jobshare.

CONSIDERING A NEW STATUS FOR A JOB

NEW STATUS	REASONS TO REVISE OLD STATUS
UPGRADED OR DOWNGRADED JOB Senior staff are expensive but can improve the effectiveness of a role. Junior staff can perform routine tasks.	● A tight budget forces a reassessment of staff costs, leading to job losses at a junior or senior level. ● A change in emphasis of the responsibilities of a job requires a different level of employee.
PART-TIME JOB The employee works for only part of the week for a period and at times agreed with the manager.	● The jobholder cites boredom as a reason for leaving, since the job does not warrant a full-time employee. ● Some tasks have become obsolete or have been reallocated among other employees.
JOBSHARE Two people share responsibility for completing tasks or achieving goals set by their supervisor.	● A valued employee can no longer work full time but wishes to remain with the organization. ● All the skills needed cannot be found in any single person within the organization.
FREELANCE POSITION A freelancer or contract worker is self-employed. They incur minimal overhead costs for an organization.	● Expected reorganization means the job is likely to change or become obsolete in the future. ● The job is necessary for a finite period only and therefore is not suitable for a full-time employee.

FINALIZING THE JOB REQUIREMENTS

*O*nce the requirements of a job have become clear, the responsibilities and tasks of the position should be detailed in a job description. The skills and experience and type of person needed for the position should then be set out in a job specification.

8 When writing a job description, do not underplay difficult aspects.

DEFINING RESPONSIBILITY

Writing an accurate job description helps ensure that the right information is given when the job is advertised, ultimately leading to a satisfactory appointment and preventing misunderstandings.

Include the title of a job and its reporting line in a description. When describing major responsibilities, set out in detail what the jobholder is expected to achieve. Use verbs of action, such as "liaise" or "develop," to describe day-to-day tasks so that you are clear about what the employee is going to do.

9 Check the salaries of similar jobs in other companies.

▼ **ASSESSING ACCURACY**
Ask the current jobholder to contribute toward redefining the job, encouraging them to be honest about any drawbacks. Discuss the reworked description with them.

CHECKING A JOB DESCRIPTION

Check that a job description contains the following elements:

- The job title;
- The reporting line of the job;
- The overall responsibilities of the job, for example "maintaining the store's reputation for attractive window dressing";
- A list of the job's chief tasks and activities, for example "serving customers from 9 a.m. to 5 p.m. on weekdays";
- Details of terms, including pay, and conditions of service.

Key personality characteristics

Experience, training, and technical skill

Special abilities, such as fluency in Tagalog

Education and formal qualifications

Mental and emotional attributes

▲ DEFINING ATTRIBUTES

When deciding on the skills you are looking for in your ideal candidate, consider the specific requirements of the job. Break the job into different areas and consider them in turn.

DEFINING SKILLS

Once you have drawn up a revised job description, you can begin to analyze the skills, qualifications, experience, and attributes needed in the person who will fill the job. This will be the job specification. Be as precise as possible: it is useful to specify what is desirable, but also what is the essential minimum, to help you assess the candidates who apply. Be realistic about what you are looking for, and keep other options open. Stating that "a knowledge of statistics is desirable" may not be possible. You may find that all candidates' statistical skills are inadequate and whomever you employ must be sent to a course.

10 Make job titles aspirational. This encourages people to grow into them.

DECIDING HOW TO RECRUIT

After drawing up a job specification, you need to choose a method of recruitment. The various methods range from advertising in the general press to using a professional headhunter. Whichever method you select will involve at least one interview.

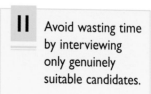

11 Avoid wasting time by interviewing only genuinely suitable candidates.

POINTS TO REMEMBER

- The response to advertisements for jobs in the general press can be overwhelming.
- Headhunters charge a percentage of the salary of the person they are recruiting, so the higher that person's salary, the more hunting they should do.
- Processing responses can be time-consuming, so a candidate should not be interviewed just on the strength of a well-written resume.

RECRUITING INTERNALLY

One way of recruiting is to appoint somebody who already works elsewhere in your organization. Many companies encourage internal recruitment, and some insist that all vacancies be advertised internally before being advertised outside.

It can be easier to interview internal applicants because they already know the company and understand its work culture. However, remember that they were originally recruited for a different job. Why are they suitable for yours? Consider also that internal recruitment may not cut costs overall. The recruit's old job may need to be filled once he or she has moved to your department.

PLACING ADVERTISEMENTS

Where you advertise and what your ad says will determine the type and number of applicants you receive and whether you find the right person for the job. Use trade publications for jobs that require specialized skills. For a more generalized approach, use the general press; some papers allocate different days to particular professions. Advertisements can be costly but usually elicit a huge response. If you lack the time or resources to cope with hundreds of applicants, advertise in a publication with limited circulation. Decide how many times you want the advertisement to appear.

12 If you know of good candidates elsewhere, invite them to apply.

DESIGNING AN ADVERTISEMENT

The design and wording of an advertisement can influence the response you get. Ensure that the layout is eye-catching and clear – size will be dictated by cost and content. Describe the job and be specific about what skills and experience are needed in order to eliminate unsuitable applicants. Always give a closing date for applications.

Introduction gives information about level of job

Headline attracts applicants' attention

Dynamic Marketing Manager

James Malcolm Associates, major operators in the computer technology market, are currently looking for a marketing manager to head up a team of three and to report directly to the general manager.

The successful candidate will manage promotion projects, adhere closely to budgets, and contribute toward new business plans for all aspects of our marketing strategy.

The successful candidate will possess a Bachelor's degree, have at least five years' relevant experience, be a team player, and be able to work under pressure.

We are an equal-opportunities employer.

Please send your resume and cover letter to:

Anna Sampson, Personnel Manager
James Malcolm Associates
53 Beech Road
North Brunswick, NJ 08902

Relevant qualifications are clearly defined

Company equal-opportunities policy is emphasized

13 Always make sure the advertisements are proofread.

Form that application should take is stated

▲ **ATTRACTING THE BEST**
Make the best features of the job prominent. You have only a moment to grab the attention of the perfect applicant!

THE LEGAL ASPECTS OF ADVERTISING

Advertising for recruitment is subject to stringent legal restrictions that vary from country to country, and from state to state in the United States. Keep in mind that your state regulations and procedures relating to employment may be different from the federal statutes and that state laws supercede federal laws. The laws most likely to apply are those of libel and those relating to discrimination on the grounds of gender, race, or age. Do not use sexist terms or refer to "he" or "him" throughout an advertisement. Select your wording carefully to avoid stipulating characteristics that exclude potential applicants of any sex or race or a particular age range, and consider stating that you are an Equal Opportunity Employer in all of your recruiting materials. If in any doubt regarding the legality of your recruiting materials, consult with your personnel office or appropriate government body.

USING RECOMMENDATIONS

There are positive and negative aspects to consider when using personal contacts to help you fill a job vacancy. On the positive side, if a potential recruit comes with a recommendation from someone you trust, it suggests that their skills and experience have, to a degree, been proved in practice. In addition, they may have been briefed by your mutual contact about the work culture within your organization. On the negative side, personal recommendations can be awkward to turn down if you feel the candidate is not right for the job. When a colleague suggests a candidate, assess their skills and abilities objectively and be prepared to reject their application if you consider them unsuitable.

14 Ask for a photograph to remind you of each candidate.

15 Be objective about a recommendation to employ a colleague's relative.

USING LOCAL RESOURCES

Check whether there are any federal or state programs in your area that are aimed at reducing unemployment levels and assisting in training. These programs are often organized on a regional basis to look at specific local needs – both of employers and the unemployed. Local universities or colleges may also employ specialized staff who deal with inquiries from prospective employers. It is a good idea to make contact with both of these resources if you have a vacancy that could be filled by a relatively inexperienced person who is looking for a first job.

Create a database of potential sources of recruits for future reference

Maintain an updated printout of the database

▲ **CREATING A LIST OF CONTACTS**
Make a list of useful contacts, including individuals, agencies, and advertisers, that you come across while recruiting. You can then use your list every time you need to fill a vacancy.

USING AGENCIES

Recruiting via an agency reduces the extensive amount of time-consuming paperwork involved in sifting through and replying to advertised vacancies. This is particularly relevant if you anticipate a substantial response. For a fee, which can vary according to the seniority of the vacancy, an agency will provide you with a shortlist of candidates from which you make the final selection. If you intend to use a recruitment agency to fill a job, ensure you approach one that can address your specific requirements. You can use professional headhunters to find suitable candidates for a senior vacancy.

16 Record the progress of each recruitment drive to use for reference in the future.

CHOOSING A METHOD OF RECRUITMENT

METHOD	FACTORS TO CONSIDER
RECRUITING INTERNALLY Initially, many employers look to recruit from internal personnel.	● Candidates have an existing track record with the company and are familiar with its way of working. ● You can ask their current manager for references.
PLACING ADVERTISEMENTS Advertisements in relevant media can reach the right candidates.	● You will need to set up a system to process what may be a large response to your advertisement. ● Advertising costs can be high.
USING RECOMMENDATIONS Friends and colleagues can provide contacts with potential candidates.	● Colleagues or acquaintances may have several contacts in the market, providing a good, informal source. ● Rejecting an unsuitable person could be problematic.
USING LOCAL RESOURCES Government agencies and colleges can be a source of recruits.	● For entry-level jobs not requiring work experience, colleges can be a good source of candidates. ● Government programs may involve extensive paperwork.
USING AGENCIES Agencies will shortlist numerous high-caliber candidates for you.	● Agencies have access to a wide range of candidates and can weed out unsuitable ones. ● There is a cost factor attached to using agencies.

SETTING UP A PROCESSING SYSTEM

Once you have decided which recruitment method (or methods) you are going to use, you need to set up an efficient response system that will enable you to deal with applications as quickly and as efficiently as possible, avoiding unnecessary delays.

17 Set minimum requirements to screen candidates.

SELECTING A PROCESS

When choosing an appropriate method for processing applications, you should consider a variety of factors. For example, will you need to process numerous application forms? Do you want to see samples of a candidate's work to assess their abilities? Do you want to follow up references before or after the interview? If you expect to receive a resume and an accompanying letter, say so in the job advertisement. Create a process that will initially divide candidates into "for interview," "possible," or "rejected."

18 Put one person in charge of all telephone applications.

IMPLEMENTING A PROCESS

Once the applicants have been sorted into three basic categories, the system for processing applications should include the following stages:

- Preparation of standard letters for rejected candidates – send these out immediately;
- Evaluation of promising candidates;
- Drawing up of a final interview list;
- Scheduling and booking interviews over the phone or by letter, confirming the date and time and stipulating if candidates will be required to take tests.

19 To speed up the process, use standard letters to respond quickly to all applicants.

DELEGATING PROCESSING

It is possible to delegate the processing of applications, but you must ensure that the person to whom you are delegating has been fully briefed. They must:

- Know the stated minimum requirements and be familiar with the job description;
- Have good organizational skills to deal with applications;
- Have time to perform the task;
- Be skilled at communicating over the phone;
- Be able to provide general background information about the company.

COPING WITH A LARGE RESPONSE

If you receive a substantial response to an advertisement, you will need to screen out the most unsuitable candidates to create a manageable number from which to select your shortlist. Do this by setting minimum criteria that all candidates must meet before you process their application any further. These criteria could include minimum educational or professional qualifications, plus a career history that includes relevant experience for a minimum period of time.

PROCESSING APPLICATIONS BEFORE THE INTERVIEWS

Decide who will deal with telephone and written inquiries
→ *Ensure your switchboard and mail room are informed*

Record the dates when responses are received
→ *If you wish to acknowledge receipt, draw up a standard letter*

File the responses under the headings "rejected," "possible," and "for interview"
→ *Send out standard letters*

Allocate blocks of time for interviewing, allowing at least an hour per interview
→ *Check availability of colleagues who are attending the interviews*

Contact candidates with interview dates and times
→ *Allocate alternative times where necessary*

Draw up a final schedule of dates, times, and candidates
→ *Distribute to colleagues who are attending the interviews*

ASSESSING A RESUME

Although most people are truthful when composing their resume, some may be tempted to omit negative facts or to exaggerate their achievements. Analyze each resume carefully to help select interviewees, then prepare questions to ask them.

20 Note specific points of interest in the resume to discuss later.

21 Assume a certain amount of creative writing in resumes.

22 Look for any inconsistencies in the facts provided.

LOOKING AT STRUCTURE

Analyzing the structure of a resume can tell you a lot about a candidate's ability to organize and communicate a set of facts effectively. A well-structured resume will be concise and normally no more than two pages in length. Usually, it will contain educational and career histories in reverse chronological order to emphasize the candidate's most recent activities. Relevant skills are often highlighted. However, there are many ways of presenting a resume, and the most important factor to consider is whether a resume presents information in a logical and easily digestible form.

READING INFORMATION

Once you have looked at the overall structure and style of a resume, examine the information provided. Consider whether the applicant's qualifications and work experience are relevant and meet the required levels you are seeking. Does the candidate have any other useful skills? Does the resume contain any background information that builds up a picture of the candidate's personality? Can you get an idea of the speed and direction of their career track?

23 Ask yourself if the format and style of the resume create a positive impression of the applicant.

DEALING WITH GAPS AND INCONSISTENCIES

Breaks in chronology and inconsistencies in the facts provided may be a result of simple error. On the negative side, however, they could provide clues to a candidate's attempt to falsify or hide certain information. You must therefore carefully examine the chronology of the applicant's educational and career achievements and ensure that all dates provided follow a logical sequence. Are there any periods of time unaccounted for? For example, is there a gap from the end of one period of employment to the beginning of the next? Does any other information supplied account for this gap? Do periods of employment overlap with periods in education? Be prepared to give applicants the benefit of the doubt, but compile a list of questions to help clarify inconsistencies.

CHECKLIST

1. Look for gaps in the resume's chronology.

2. If necessary, verify qualifications with relevant institutions.

3. Estimate the average amount of time spent in each job.

4. Judge whether the candidate is making a logical career move.

5. Consider if the style of the resume indicates a well-organized candidate.

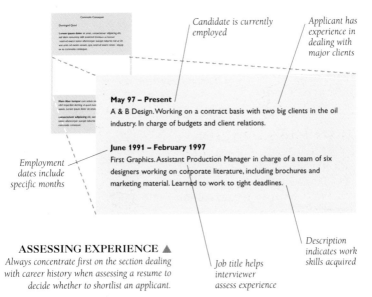

Candidate is currently employed

Applicant has experience in dealing with major clients

May 97 – Present
A & B Design. Working on a contract basis with two big clients in the oil industry. In charge of budgets and client relations.

June 1991 – February 1997
First Graphics. Assistant Production Manager in charge of a team of six designers working on corporate literature, including brochures and marketing material. Learned to work to tight deadlines.

Employment dates include specific months

Description indicates work skills acquired

ASSESSING EXPERIENCE ▲
Always concentrate first on the section dealing with career history when assessing a resume to decide whether to shortlist an applicant.

Job title helps interviewer assess experience

CONSIDERING APPLICATIONS

When considering the applications you have received, divide the criteria of the job specification into those that are essential and those that are desirable. Are there other attributes – in terms of personality or physical skills – that you are looking for?

24 Application forms create a level playing field for all candidates.

USING YOUR CRITERIA

25 Seek the advice of colleagues when considering borderline cases.

Before deciding on candidates to shortlist for interview, take the job specification and divide the criteria into essential and merely desirable. For example, how important is it that the recruit can speak one or more foreign languages? Should they have computer skills, or are you willing to provide training if they do not? Ideal candidates who can fulfill all your criteria will be rare, so you must be prepared to be flexible at the selection stage.

CONSIDERING YOUR CRITERIA

INTERVIEWER
By the time you are considering applications, you should have decided which of your criteria are essential and which are merely preferable.

EXAMPLES OF CRITERIA
- Education: What level of educational attainment are you looking for? Would you consider a high-school graduate, or is it essential to have a graduate degree?
- Work experience: Are you looking for specific work skills acquired through employment? Should the applicants bring with them a range of valuable new contacts for your company?
- Information technology skills: Are basic computer skills absolutely essential? Does your company use specific software packages that any new recruit must be thoroughly familiar with, or are you willing to invest in training?
- Communicating and negotiating skills: Should the candidate be an effective communicator and experienced negotiator?
- Travel: Does the candidate need to travel on a regular basis and for prolonged periods?

TALKING TO COLLEAGUES

Before you reject borderline candidates it may be useful to discuss their applications with colleagues whose opinions you trust or who will work with the new person. Objective second opinions may help you decide to interview a seemingly unsuitable candidate who is in fact right for the job. Colleagues may also know of other opportunities for which the candidate could be considered.

DISCUSSING APPLICANTS ▶
Discuss borderline candidates with your workmates. They may highlight some positive qualities that you have missed.

REJECTING CANDIDATES

When rejecting a candidate, use a courteous and professional tone. Remember that each applicant is likely to have invested a considerable amount of time and effort in applying for the job. Send a polite letter as soon as possible, thanking each candidate for their interest. Point out that although their application has not been successful this time, you will keep their details on file should any other suitable vacancies arise in the future.

26 Be courteous and positive when replying to all rejected applicants.

ANALYZING APPLICATION FORMS

Application forms are helpful when it comes to assessing candidates since they put all interviewees on the same footing – each candidate is required to answer the same set of questions. When considering an application form, it is relatively straightforward to compare candidates equally against the criteria and make a selection for interview. You can use the information provided to create a database, which can be used for future reference, and to build up a profile of the range and skills of applicants. This will make it easier for you to select individuals who are skilled in the specific areas in which you are trying to fill vacancies.

SELECTING INTERVIEWEES

*O*nce you have assessed applicants, you
*can start to draw up a shortlist of
interviewees. Often, only a small number
of candidates are suitable – if this is not so,
choosing whom to interview from the shortlist
can be the hardest part of the exercise.*

27 Screen applicants
by meeting them
informally before
holding interviews.

USING A MATCHING SHEET

28 Decide if you need
to hold written
tests to filter
out candidates.

One technique for deciding whom to shortlist is
to create a "matching sheet" for each candidate.
Take a blank sheet of paper and draw two lines
down the middle. On one side, list the criteria
required for the job; make copies of the sheet and
use one per applicant, noting their skills and
experience on the blank side. In the center column,
check off the items that match for each candidate,
then select those with the most checks to interview.

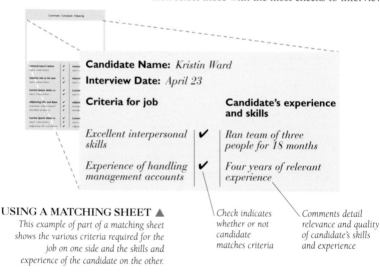

Candidate Name: *Kristin Ward*

Interview Date: *April 23*

Criteria for job

**Candidate's experience
and skills**

*Excellent interpersonal
skills* ✔ *Ran team of three
people for 18 months*

*Experience of handling
management accounts* ✔ *Four years of relevant
experience*

USING A MATCHING SHEET ▲
*This example of part of a matching sheet
shows the various criteria required for the
job on one side and the skills and
experience of the candidate on the other.*

*Check indicates
whether or not
candidate
matches criteria*

*Comments detail
relevance and quality
of candidate's skills
and experience*

**CHECKING ▶
DETAILS**
*If you call a candidate
to check their details,
first ask whether it is
convenient for them
to talk to you.*

*Points checked
off as they are
confirmed*

CHECKING DETAILS

If you want to confirm some of the details of a candidate's resume, there are several ways to go about it. You may want to contact their school or university to check details of their education, but be sure that the candidate is aware that you are going to do so at this early stage. Alternatively, telephone the candidate at his or her office. Always remember to check that they can talk freely and are not constrained by being within hearing distance of their current boss or colleagues.

POINTS TO REMEMBER

● Some applicants claim that their current salary is more than it is.

● It is harder to lie in person, even over the telephone, than in a written application.

● If applicable, ask candidates if they are willing to relocate.

● If it is not possible to contact candidates' references immediately, it may initially be necessary to trust what candidates say.

● Although humor is a valuable quality, you should expect a candidate to be serious during the interview.

● Instinctive reactions from speaking to candidates on the phone are worth noting.

ESTABLISHING A SHORTLIST TO INTERVIEW

Your shortlist of candidates selected to interview should not be so long that your impressions of them will blur into one another when interviewing. You need, of course, to include the candidates who appear at this stage to be your first choice plus a reserve or reserves. These should be those with the closest fit to the requirements of the job in terms of their skills and achievements.

On the shortlist, you might want also to include one or two who have exceptional skills in specific areas but who have shortcomings as all-arounders. Depending on the post you are trying to fill, it may be worth interviewing a couple of unconventional candidates. If the job requires making radical changes, the most suitable person is unlikely to be the one who is most familiar with the aspects that need to be revolutionized.

ARRANGING INTERVIEWS

It may be difficult to arrange interviews with all the shortlisted candidates in a short space of time. Many will need to take time off from their current jobs or to travel a considerable distance. Bear this in mind, and be as flexible as possible in scheduling.

29 Be prepared to schedule some interviews outside office hours.

30 Offer refreshments to candidates in order to help put them at ease.

STAGING INTERVIEWS

Before arranging any interviews, clarify how long the whole process will take. The level of vacancy may dictate how many stages you need: for a junior position, one interview may be enough to reach a decision, but for a more senior post you may want to ask some candidates for a second interview. Make arrangements and allow time for any tests that may need to be carried out. Confirm all details of the interviews in writing to the candidates, and send travel instructions to them.

CHOOSING INTERVIEWERS

In certain circumstances, it is desirable to invite specific colleagues to participate in the process of selecting a new employee. In some companies, a member of the personnel department is required to attend all interviews. This is especially valuable if the vacant position is a senior one or if the interviewer is inexperienced. If an employee will be working for more than one person, try to make sure that all those to whom the jobholder will report are present. Consider asking your own superiors if they wish to attend, especially if the position is a key one within your team. If the employee will be working closely with another department, invite one of its representatives to help assess the prospective new team members.

POINTS TO REMEMBER

- Having a colleague join you during the interview can provide a valuable second opinion.
- A perceptive receptionist can offer invaluable insights into candidates' attitudes.
- Candidates should be allowed time to ask questions and perhaps be shown around the office.
- The shorter the shortlist, the shorter the time it is likely to take to fill a position.
- Candidates should not be kept waiting or in an interview longer than necessary. It may be difficult for them to be away from work.

CHOOSING WHO WILL ATTEND THE INTERVIEW

INTERVIEWER	FACTORS TO CONSIDER
MANAGER Another manager for whom the employee will be working.	● Any manager to whom the new employee will report will need to be involved in the selection process to help avoid future dissatisfaction. ● A manager who is a more experienced interviewer than you may suggest useful interviewing techniques and provide a valuable second opinion.
COLLEAGUE A representative of a department with which the employee will work closely.	● Factors pertinent to work that needs to be done with another department will need to be evaluated by a representative of that department. ● A colleague does not have the authority to make the final selection of candidate or to negotiate the terms and conditions of employment.
SUPERIOR The manager to whom you report who authorizes the appointment.	● Your superior may wish to be involved in the selection process if you are inexperienced. ● The overall "fit" of candidates within the team or department may be best assessed by your superior. ● Your superior may need to meet the candidate before a final offer can be made.

SCHEDULING AND TIMING INTERVIEWS

Make alternative dates and times available for holding interviews in case candidates are unable to attend on suggested days. Schedule interviews with a generous amount of time between them. It can be embarrassing for candidates to bump into their rivals outside. This may make them nervous and unlikely to give their best. Allowing some space between interviews will allow you to spend more time with a candidate if you wish or to run over if there is a delay. It should also mean that you have plenty of time to write up detailed notes on each candidate – a stream of interviewees tends to blur indistinguishably as soon as the interviews are over. Finally, take a brief rest to recharge yourself.

31 Be sure to avoid all interruptions during interviews.

32 Get plenty of rest so that you can be alert during an interview.

LOCATING INTERVIEWS

Give careful thought to the location of interviews: this can have a material effect on the proceedings. Remember that you are interviewing to get the best candidate for the position, but interviewees will find it hard to give their best if they are uncomfortable.

33 Put a "Do not disturb" notice on the door of the interview room.

CHOOSING A LOCATION

You need to decide whether it is best to hold the interview in your workplace or on neutral territory somewhere else. If you use your workplace, do you want to hold it in your own office, or in a more clinical meeting room? If you need privacy or secrecy, then choose neutral ground, such as a hotel room, or the office of a third party. Try to create a relaxing atmosphere with comfortable seats and lighting that is not too harsh.

BEING AWARE OF ▼ THE ATMOSPHERE

While conducting an interview, avoid all distractions and concentrate on putting candidates at ease. This will help them perform at their best.

Candidate feels intimidated due to sitting on a low chair

Computer screen is a distraction

Telephone may ring and interrupt interview

ARRANGING SEATING

There are several different ways to arrange seating at an interview. Sitting face to face is always a more formal option, while sitting side by side creates a more informal, cooperative atmosphere. If you decide on the face-to-face option, remember that people generally prefer to have some kind of solid surface such as a table between them, since sitting with their knees exposed can make interviewees feel even more awkward and vulnerable. Unless it is part of your intentional strategy, do not seat candidates on a chair that is lower than yours – this may make them feel inferior and uncomfortable.

34 Indicate where you would like the interviewee to sit.

35 Provide clear directions to the interview room.

Key

Interviewer   Candidate

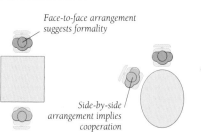

Face-to-face arrangement suggests formality

Side-by-side arrangement implies cooperation

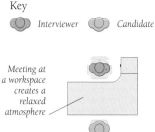

Meeting at a workspace creates a relaxed atmosphere

▲ FORMAL INTERVIEW

A square or a rectangular table is more formal than a small, round table.

▲ INFORMAL INTERVIEW

A large, round table creates an informal atmosphere and can seat more than two people.

▲ INTERVIEW IN YOUR OFFICE

Using your own workspace is informal. It is often appropriate for internal candidates.

DO'S AND DON'TS

☑ Do pull blinds so that nobody gets dazzled.

☑ Do take the phone off the hook during the interview.

☑ Do ensure the room is well ventilated and that neither of you is too hot or too cold.

☒ Don't let the interviewee see your notes or the contents of your files.

☒ Don't hang distracting images on your wall.

☒ Don't offer food. Neither of you can eat and talk properly.

Panel sits in line facing candidate

▲ PANEL INTERVIEW

Sitting on opposite sides of a rectangular table is confrontational, which may be appropriate for formal interviews.

DECIDING ON STRATEGY

The most important decision to make before an interview is what its style should be. Do you want to keep it factual, or do you want to put the candidate under pressure? The answer to this may depend on the job for which you are interviewing.

36 Allow time before a panel interview for everyone to agree on objectives.

CONSIDERING YOUR AIMS

Keeping your criteria for the job in mind, consider what you want to achieve in the interview. Select a strategy that will help you. If you know the interviewee's technical skills are right for the job, you may choose to concentrate on their people skills in the interview. Alternatively, you may adopt an aggressive interview style to test the candidate's reactions under pressure.

37 Give all the interviewers full details of all the candidates.

PREPARING AN INTERVIEW STRATEGY

STYLE OF INTERVIEW	HOW TO PREPARE
FACTUAL The main point is to extract factual information. The candidate's personality is less important.	Compile a list of general and specific questions designed to come up with the answers that you need.
SITUATIONAL The aim of a situational interview is to see how the candidate handles key parts of the job.	Prepare open questions such as, "What would you do if...?" Lead interviewees into a full description of the ensuing scenario.
CONFRONTATIONAL Use a confrontational style to gauge how the interviewee behaves under work-related stress.	Plan a confrontation that makes attacks on and insinuations about the interviewee's track record and career progression.
TECHNICAL Use a technical interview to establish that the candidate has the skills that they claim to have.	Set up a practical test, for example selling something to a colleague or manipulating software on your computer.

STRUCTURING INTERVIEWS

Exactly what your interview will consist of depends on your strategy. However, it is usual for interviews to exist as variations of the following:

● An introduction and a "getting to know you" phase where you talk about generalities;

● A question-and-answer session to fill in any gaps in the candidate's resume;

● An investigation of the candidate's character and personal qualities;

● A final stage where the candidate asks questions about the job and its terms and conditions.

You can adapt these to your strategy – for example, you may want to include a technical test. When using aggressive tactics, you might omit the introductory phase.

38 If teamwork is important, set group exercises for the candidates.

39 Structure the interview to suit your strategy.

INTERVIEWING BY PANEL

A panel interview has the advantage of allowing several interviewers to assess a candidate simultaneously. The interplay of their questions can elicit far more than any one line of questioning on its own. Panel interviews also take some of the pressure – and therefore the stress – from the individual interviewer. A decision is reached based on the opinions of several people after conferring. Make sure that the balance of panel members is equal and that no single member dominates the interview. You may choose interviewers based on their areas of expertise, or because they will be working with the successful candidate. Role playing between the panelists is a popular strategy.

Interviewer asks hostile questions

Interviewer adopts friendly approach

▲ **DECIDING ON ROLE PLAYING**
An interview panel can divide the questions between them. Alternatively, two interviewers may play the roles of hostile interviewer and friendly interviewer.

PREPARING QUESTIONS

Your main chance to find out information about a candidate comes from asking the right questions in the right way. Phrase questions carefully to obtain the details that you want. Use the interviewee's answers to lead into your next question.

40 Start an interview with easy questions to help relax the candidate.

41 Modify your list of questions for each of the candidates you interview.

QUESTIONS TO ASK AN APPLICANT

Q Why do you want to change jobs at this point?

Q What do you consider your greatest attributes?

Q What have your relationships been like with past employers?

Q What for you has been the highlight of your career so far?

Q What has been the low point of your career so far?

Q What experience do you have with problem-solving?

Q What are your long-term goals, and how do you think you can achieve them here?

UNDERSTANDING HOW TO PHRASE QUESTIONS

You can manipulate a candidate's answers by phrasing your questions in different ways. Open questions are likely to be the most useful in an interview. They encourage the candidate to open up, think, and talk at length, and enable you to observe a candidate's communication skills and elicit detailed information. These questions usually start with words such as "What?", "When?", "Why?", and "How?" – "How did you first become interested in tropical hardwoods?" Open questions may also start with a statement about yourself and then follow with a question – "I once went to the botanical gardens in Sydney. Which gardens have you been to?"

Closed questions lead to a simple affirmative or negative, rather than an in-depth reply. Use them to clarify unclear points, for example, "Can we expect you to begin the job on November 14th?" These questions are also useful for seeking confirmation of details of a candidate's resume.

42 Ask "open" questions – that is, those that invite more than a simple "yes" or "no" answer.

UNDERSTANDING "LOADED" QUESTIONS

A loaded question is one that makes the candidate react to a deliberate assumption about them. For example, test how close the candidate is to accepting a job by saying, "When do you think you can go to our Munich office?" If the candidate's response is "Aren't we jumping the gun?", you know you still have some way to go. However, if he or she seems eager, you can assume that you are near a deal. Avoid asking these questions in an aggressive tone.

Tilted head indicates a lack of trust

Crossed legs and clasped hands imply defensiveness

TAILORING QUESTIONS ▶

When interviewing, avoid asking questions that make the candidate clam up or act defensively. Watch their body language for signs of defensive behavior.

USING A CHECKLIST

It can be useful to have a prepared checklist of questions that you want to ask in an interview. However, do not stick too rigidly to either the order or the content of the list – an interview is a two-way communication. The main purposes of the checklist are to provide the security that comes from knowing that you have covered all the ground and to have a list to refer to if necessary.

> **43** Use closed questions only if you require a specific response.

BUILDING ON QUESTIONS

The interviewer's questions must be influenced by the interviewee's answers. Each question should build on the one before to steer the candidate toward providing you with the information you need. "So you decided to take a six-month break?"… "Did you travel immediately?"… "Why did you decide to wait so long before leaving?"… "How long did it take you to get a job when you returned?"… "So you spent two weeks in Asia and five months looking for a job. Is that correct?"

> **44** Use a candidate's resume and matching sheet to generate interview questions.

HONING LISTENING SKILLS

Attentive listening is one of the most essential abilities of an interviewer. If you appear to be listening, your interviewee will be encouraged to keep talking. Work at keeping your concentration focused and becoming aware of your body language.

45 You have two ears and one mouth – listen twice as much as you talk.

46 Summarize what a candidate is saying to show that you are listening.

ANALYZING YOUR SKILLS

Most people like the the sound of their own voice yet also believe that they are good listeners. Try this test to find out how good a listener you are. Tape-record a conversation with a colleague, then listen to it objectively. Who talks more? Who talks faster? Do you respond to your colleague's concerns or merely continue what you were saying before you were interrupted? By analyzing the tape, you will be able to hear in which areas you need to improve, as well as in which areas you are strong.

PRACTICING ▼ BODY LANGUAGE
Learn to use positive body language as part of your preparations. Here, the interviewer is focusing attentively on what the candidate is saying.

Interviewer's expression is open and attentive

Leaning forward indicates interest

AVOIDING BAD HABITS

Even good listeners develop bad habits. Two of the most common ones are "turning off" to information that you are not interested in, and interrupting people before they have finished what they are saying. If you know that you are prone to these habits, make an effort to overcome them. Remember, developing a good listening technique requires awareness, practice, and effort.

 47 Keep checking with a candidate that you have understood everything you have been told.

THINGS TO DO

1. Be curious. It helps you listen properly.
2. Ensure you understand a question before answering.
3. Jot down questions as they occur to you, leaving your mind free to listen.
4. Listen to the emotions behind the words.
5. Correct any bad listening habits that you have.

BEING AWARE OF NEGATIVE BODY LANGUAGE

There is a clear distinction between hearing and listening. Make yourself aware of any negative body language you may use when you are not fully concentrating. Once you are aware, you can consciously avoid lapsing into bad habits in an interview.

Interviewer's closed body language implies a closed mind

◀ **BEING DEFENSIVE**

This man is sitting in a defensive position. If you adopt a pose such as this – crossed arms and leaning backward – the candidate will feel you are not receptive to what is said.

Interviewer has chin in hand, indicating contemplation

BEING ▶
INATTENTIVE
This interviewer appears contemplative and unfocused on the interview. This may be interpreted negatively by the interviewee as a lack of enthusiasm in her application.

PREPARING YOURSELF

Just before an interview begins, make a last-minute check that you have all the information you need, that any equipment (such as a tape recorder) is working smoothly, and that you are informed about the subject matter and in a positive frame of mind.

48 Be prepared to answer some questions as well as to ask them.

PREPARING YOUR TOOLS

49 Make a checklist to take into the interview with you.

Decide how you are going to keep a record of the interview. Note-taking is the usual method. It is discreet, but it takes up your time and may divert your attention from the interview. If you are going to take notes, use a notepad rather than scribbling in the margins of a resume, which you may later need to show to somebody else. An alternative method is taping an interview. Although this frees you to concentrate on the interview, it may make the interviewee nervous. Always check that your tape recorder has enough batteries and spare tape to last for the duration of the interview.

50 Ask a candidate's permission before taping an interview.

PRESENTING YOURSELF

Remember that you are an ambassador, selling your organization to a candidate almost as much as they are selling themselves to you. Ensure that you look neat and presentable and are appropriately dressed. If you are recruiting for a laid-back company in which employees usually wear casual clothes, reflect this in your dress. If you are recruiting for a formal organization, dress more soberly.

You will need to be well informed about your company. Gather all the relevant details, and be ready to answer candidates' questions. You may also want to give candidates printed information or copies of the company's annual report.

51 Straighten your clothing and make sure your hair is neat just before starting an interview.

PREPARING YOUR MATERIAL

There is a range of information you should have at your fingertips in an interview, including the following:

● What does the job involve, generally and specifically?

● To whom will the new employee report?

● What salary can you offer, and when will it be reviewed?

● Is there any opportunity (or need) to work overtime?

● What are the prospects for promotion?

● What are the perks that go with the job – such as pension, health insurance, and vacation time?

Interviewer reviews key resume points

Resume and application letter give details of experience

▲ **CHECKING OVER MATERIAL**
Immediately before an interview, take another quick look at a candidate's resume. Make sure that your list of prepared questions will elicit the information you want to obtain.

FOCUSING FOR FIVE MINUTES

Five or ten minutes before a candidate is due to arrive (and you should assume that he or she will be on time, if not a little early), go over their papers. Remind yourself of the questions that you want to ask and the order in which you intend asking them. Focus on the sort of person you are looking for, and try to erase the image of other candidates from your mind. Then relax for a minute or two. Lean back in your chair, arms at your side, and breathe in deeply. Exhale slowly and evenly, and repeat several times. You will feel refreshed and ready for the next candidate.

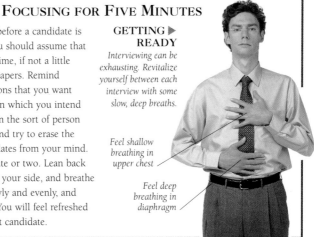

GETTING ▶ READY
Interviewing can be exhausting. Revitalize yourself between each interview with some slow, deep breaths.

Feel shallow breathing in upper chest

Feel deep breathing in diaphragm

CONDUCTING AN INTERVIEW

Interviews can be nerve-wracking for interviewers as well as candidates. Conduct them in a way that puts both parties at ease to maximize what you glean from your meeting.

OPENING AN INTERVIEW

The first few moments of an interview are vitally important: this is when initial impressions are formed. Whatever your status, greet each candidate with the same politeness and respect you would want to receive if the roles were reversed.

52 If interviewees arrive early, let them know when you can see them.

CULTURAL DIFFERENCES

Be aware of cultural differences when greeting interviewees: in some cultures, men greet each other with an embrace and a kiss on the cheek; in others, men and women alike simply bow. The handshake, in various forms, is almost universally accepted and is generally the safest option.

GREETING A CANDIDATE

An effective greeting can make all the difference. Stand up when an interviewee arrives, make eye contact, smile, and move forward to give a firm (but not bone-crunching) handshake. Welcome the candidate by name. If there are others in the room, introduce them clearly and repeat their names later on in case the interviewee has forgotten them. Ask the interviewee to sit down, then offer something to drink – this is especially important if the candidate has traveled some distance to meet you. Remember: however nervous you are, the candidate is sure to be more so.

Candidate meets interviewer's eye, suggesting confidence and honesty

Interviewer and candidate shake hands, establishing good will

Interviewer makes direct eye contact

Interviewer leans forward, implying eagerness to meet

Interviewer stands in polite acknowledgment of candidate's arrival

RELAXING A CANDIDATE

There are times in everyone's life when people temporarily lose whatever leadership qualities they may have and wait to be told what to do. Walking into a room to be interviewed is one such occasion. When interviewing, take the initiative in order to help candidates feel at ease. Go through a formal process of asking candidates to sit down and showing them to their seats. Try to avoid embarrassing them. For example, if a candidate misjudges the appropriate level of formality of dress, or spills some coffee, play such matters down when the opportunity arises.

▲ ESTABLISHING AN INSTANT RAPPORT
Create a positive rapport with the candidate by standing to greet him. Lean toward the candidate and make eye contact to encourage him to relax.

53 Smile, but do not overdo it; this will make you appear nervous.

EVALUATING AN APPLICANT

The most important aim of conducting an interview is to form an impression of a candidate's personality and abilities. To do this, you must supplement the information gained from the resume, so ask perceptive questions and take note of your impressions.

54 Remember that the "best" candidate may just be good at interviews.

55 Dress in a way that will not distract your candidate.

CONSIDERING IMPRESSIONS

Before the interview begins in earnest, you will have already formed an impression of the candidate. Be aware of any prejudices that might color your first impression: perhaps you are adversely affected by long hair, by a particular accent, or by a style of dress. Similarly, the interviewee will have formed an opinion about your company. An unfavorable impression is hard to change once formed, so it is your responsibility to give a good impression of yourself and your company.

56 Behave as close to natural as possible when interviewing.

If possible, start the interview with friendly conversation to make both of you feel at ease. It can be about general subjects such as the weather, your office's location, recent news events, or any subject that you both have in common.

COVERING ALL THE FACTS

Besides getting an overall impression of the candidate's character, you need to check the facts in the resume. Ask detailed questions about education, work experience, and other job-related skills. You may uncover useful things – for example, that the candidate speaks a second language because a parent was born in a foreign country. Interviewees may possess skills that they themselves thought irrelevant but you recognize as having potential.

57 Ask yourself if the candidate is both able and willing to do the job.

LOOKING AT CAREER PROGRESSION

To assess whether candidates are applying for a job to further their careers or whether they want the job for other reasons, ask them how they see their careers developing. If you are interviewing for a company that is often used as a stepping stone by ambitious young people, make sure the candidates' aims relate to the company's aims. Even if people stay with your organization for just a short time, you may benefit enough from their talents to make it worth employing them.

SPOTTING GAPS

If there are gaps in a candidate's employment history, it is important to find out the reasons for them. Remember that not all gaps are the result of involuntary unemployment. They may have occurred because of prolonged illness, travel, taking time off to have children, or looking after ailing parents. Even those gaps that are the result of unemployment may not reflect badly on the candidates themselves. Ask the candidates open-ended questions about any gaps and why they occurred. You may find that they were let go or left a job for good reasons. Focus on how the candidate used the time between periods of paid employment.

58 Avoid asking personal questions that are irrelevant to the job.

PAYING ATTENTION ▶ TO DETAIL
Look out for career progression or continuity in a particular area of work. Do the candidate's interests reflect any requirements for this job?

ASSESSING ABILITIES

In certain cases, the extent of a candidate's qualifications may be sufficient to gauge his or her ability to do the job, assuming that the qualifications are appropriate and have been kept up to date. In most cases, however, relevant or associated work experience is considered to be a more valuable indication of skill and aptitude. Your job as an interviewer is to assess the candidate's professional, technical, and practical abilities using all the information available to you.

 59 Jot down values for the relevant abilities of a candidate.

ASSESSING A CANDIDATE'S SKILLS

SKILLS	WAYS TO ASSESS SKILLS
ORGANIZATIONAL Does the candidate display signs of being well organized and methodical?	Ask about the candidate's attitude toward being organized. Find out about preferences for filing systems, and ask how the candidate might start to organize a hypothetical project.
ANALYTICAL How well can the candidate analyze business situations, and how quickly can they come up with the best solutions?	Ask for examples of their problem-solving ability. Describe a difficult situation, and ask them to pick out the key points and come up with a potential solution.
DECISION-MAKING How well can the candidate make difficult decisions, and how quickly can they then implement those decisions?	Ask about their previous experience. What difficult decisions have they had to make in the past? How did they reach the decision? How well did they handle the repercussions?
SOCIAL Will the candidate get on well with the superiors, colleagues, and subordinates with whom he or she will be working?	Ask about the candidate's experience of teamwork. Do they prefer to work alone or in a team? Ask them how they would handle a hypothetical problem with a colleague.
COMMUNICATION How efficient is the candidate at communicating clearly and confidently?	Assess the candidate's verbal skills from the interview itself, then ask about written ability. Have they written lengthy reports? Can you see them?

ASSESSING PERSONALITY

The candidate's attitude toward colleagues and the workplace is determined by their personality; their personality also affects their relationships with colleagues and the atmosphere of the workplace.

Try to assess whether a candidate will fit in with the culture of your organization, and find out about the work culture of the candidate's previous companies. For example, a work culture that encourages team spirit will not suit someone who comes from a background of intense internal competition where "creative tension" has been positively encouraged. Has the candidate always worked in small companies where everyone knows what is going on? If yours is a large organization, how will they cope with not knowing the details of company business and decision-making? In addition, think about the balance of current staff. Do you need, for example, a specific personality type such as an extrovert to balance a rather introverted team, or vice versa?

60 Note when a candidate responds with enthusiasm – this can tell you what motivates them.

ACTING AS AN AMBASSADOR

Remember that as you are assessing the candidate, so the candidate is assessing you and the organization you work for. There is a shortage of potential employees in many areas and, in these cases, you need to work hard to attract high-caliber recruits. This means that when you meet a candidate for the first time, you are acting as an ambassador for your company. Do this by letting the candidate know that you are prepared to go to considerable trouble and expense to find the right person for the job. Show that you are genuinely interested in achieving this and that when they come to work for the company they will be a valued staff member.

QUESTIONS TO ASK AN APPLICANT

Q What do you think you could bring to this job?

Q What do you regard as the main achievement in your life?

Q What are you looking for first and foremost in a job?

Q Where do you see yourself in five years' time?

Q How do you handle the pressure of deadlines?

Q Do you like working as part of a team, or do you prefer working on projects alone?

Q How do you think your best friend would describe you?

61 Give positive feedback to encourage in-depth discussion.

CONTROLLING AN INTERVIEW

P*ace an interview carefully so that you can cover all the necessary ground in the time allocated. You must be able to direct a candidate gently toward another subject if required, or hurry them along politely if they linger too long on a favorite topic.*

62 Allow a few minutes for small talk before the interview.

POINTS TO REMEMBER

- Talking too much initially may be a symptom of nervousness.
- Initial stuttering and stumbling over words and phrases may also be a sign of nerves.
- Talking directly to the point shows that the candidate is listening to you attentively.
- It is not necessarily a bad sign if a candidate shows some emotion during the interview.

CONTROLLING THE FLOW OF INFORMATION

Try to control the flow of information during an interview. For example, give supportive feedback to encourage a candidate to discuss sensitive issues. Say "It must have been very difficult for you to let those people go" to draw out more detail of how the situation was handled. Although you should always try to cover most of your planned questions, do not stick rigidly to them if a candidate has something unexpected to say on a subject that affects their application.

USING SILENCE TACTICALLY

Use silence tactically during an interview. Do not prolong it to such an extent that it makes the interviewee uncomfortable, but do let it run whenever a candidate is obviously searching for words or thinking about an answer. Note how candidates respond to silence – do they rush to fill the vacuum with hasty, ill-thought-out remarks, or do they have the confidence to take the time that they need to frame a coherent answer to a difficult or complicated question?

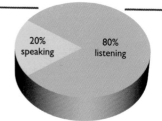

▲ **LISTENING PROPERLY**
Speak for 20 percent of the time in an interview and listen to the candidate speak for the other 80 percent of the session.

HANDLING CANDIDATES

The personalities of candidates who have the same qualifications will vary enormously – one may be seemingly in control, another a bag of nerves. You will be able judge their relative merits only if you know how they all respond to certain situations. Ask all your candidates roughly the same questions – for example, probe their ability to handle crisis situations at work – to see how different their reactions are. If interviewees do become flustered when responding to your questioning, try gently to calm them down; ask another question that leads away from the topic that appears to be causing them discomfort.

63 Respect candidates who can admit that they do not know an answer.

64 If your interviewee becomes flustered, stay calm yourself.

Making direct eye contact reassures interviewee

Leaning forward shows attentiveness

Open hands help calm interviewee

Hands are raised protectively to face

Facial expression shows distress

▲ **CALMING A DISTRESSED CANDIDATE**
If someone is having difficulty in explaining a particular point, introduce a new topic and come back to the original point later.

READING BODY LANGUAGE

Learn to read people's body language. It may convey as much about them as their words do. Body language is particularly useful to an interviewer – it is difficult for a candidate to be evasive or dishonest using body language because it is instinctive.

65 Mirror body language to establish a good rapport.

WATCHING A CANDIDATE

66 Train yourself to notice people's body language automatically.

Look at a candidate's body language while he or she is speaking. Do the candidate's words match what they are "saying" with their body? For example, is their posture hunched and defensive even as they are claiming they are "good with people"? In particular, observe the candidate's eyes. Are they averted unconsciously at times when you would expect to have eye contact?

CONTROLLING YOUR BODY LANGUAGE

Be aware of your own body language, and try to avoid giving adverse signals. Certain postures and gestures of the interviewer can give negative signals and may discourage a candidate from continuing to give out information.

Hand stifles yawn

▲ BOREDOM

Yawning during an interview will give the impression of boredom. It may, however, be due to nerves.

Facial expression glazed, with slight smirk

Hands fiddling

▲ INATTENTION

Avoid fiddling or looking distracted, since this may indicate that you are preoccupied with other matters.

Looking at watch

▲ IMPATIENCE

If you often look at your watch a candidate may think you wish to be elsewhere, even if this is not so.

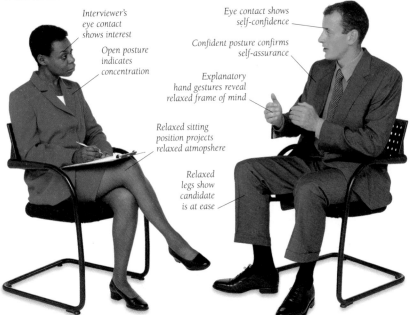

Interviewer's
eye contact
shows interest

Open posture
indicates
concentration

Eye contact shows
self-confidence

Confident posture confirms
self-assurance

Explanatory
hand gestures reveal
relaxed frame of mind

Relaxed sitting
position projects
relaxed atmopshere

Relaxed
legs show
candidate
is at ease

READING POSITIVE SIGNS

A person who is grinning broadly is giving off a very positive signal, while one whose eyes are fixed to the floor is giving off a very negative signal. However, positive signals are not always so blatant. A confident person will tend to sit upright, or with their body leaning slightly forward, even when being interviewed by their potential future boss. When confident candidates are not speaking, their legs and arms usually remain quite still and they tend to make both frequent and firm eye contact.

Shaking hands with a candidate can give you an immediate impression of their frame of mind. If they are relaxed and comfortable, their hands will be warm and dry. However, cold, sweaty hands indicate nervousness.

▲ GOOD RAPPORT

These two people are clearly in tune with each other: all aspects of their body language are open, relaxed, and attentive.

CULTURAL DIFFERENCES

Different cultures have different norms of body language and personal space. In some, people are open and tactile, even with strangers; in others, people will feel invaded if you sit or stand too close. If you are unsure, ask an experienced colleague for advice.

- Nervousness – and yawning – can be contagious, so it is important to remember that a candidate may be mirroring your own body language.

- A candidate's body language may contradict what he or she is saying verbally.

- Speaking slowly tends to indicate that one is at ease. Speaking quickly may be a sign of being nervous or of great enthusiasm.

READING SUBTLE SIGNS

There are many subtle clues to a person's frame of mind. Pay attention to the position of their body, their arms and legs, and their eyes.

Note, too, their tone of voice. This will strongly affect the way they are perceived. If you are filling a managerial post or a job that involves dealing with the press, for example, bear in mind that someone with a squeaky, high-pitched voice may find it difficult to command attention and respect. On the other hand, they may sound high-pitched on this occasion only because of nerves.

SEEING NERVOUS SIGNALS

Develop your ability to spot nervousness. Common signs include foot-tapping, rubbing the nose or lips with the back of the hand, wringing the hands, fiddling with a writing implement, or tearing up a tissue – if a candidate does any of these, consider the possibility that they may be very nervous. Note, too, if they smile too much, which may indicate an excessive desire to be liked. If an interviewee is unable to establish eye contact – to look you straight in the eye – you can deduce that they are probably ill at ease. But treat such observations as no more than clues to alert you to points to watch for – apparent nervous behavior may have several other explanations.

67 Watch hand movements – they can give a lot away.

Lips are touched in an unconscious form of comfort-seeking

Hands are crossed over body in a defensive manner

Legs are rigid

◀ **NERVOUS CANDIDATE**
The position of this candidate's feet indicates that he is not at ease. This is further reinforced by the position of his hands: one touching his lips, the other held across his body.

68 Listen to your candidate's voice: a high pitch may indicate nerves.

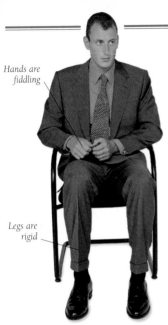

Hands are fiddling

Legs are rigid

SPOTTING EVASIVENESS

Be aware of the signs that candidates are trying to evade a question – either because they do not know how to answer or because their answer might reveal something that they would rather hide. A range of body language may give them away:

● Avoiding eye contact;
● Talking around the question, and including lots of jargon to confuse you;
● Fidgeting, or playing with their hair or with any implement, such as a pen.

◀ **EVASIVE CANDIDATE**
This man's posture shows that he is ill at ease. His body and legs are stiff, and he is fiddling with his hands and looking around him in order to avoid eye contact.

Hand gestures are expansive

Arm is hooked casually over chair arm

RECOGNIZING ARROGANCE

While most candidates at job interviews are nervous and need to be put at ease, a few seem to be overconfident to the extent of being arrogant. They tend to speak rather than listen and to speak at length, giving the impression that they like the sound of their own voice. This behavior may be because they feel they are too good for the job, or perhaps they are overcompensating for lack of self-confidence. Either way, contain such candidates by maintaining a formal interviewing style and asking a series of brisk, difficult questions. They may rise to the challenge – or become defensive.

ARROGANT CANDIDATE ▶
This candidate's body language suggests that he is arrogant. He is sprawled in the chair in an overconfident way, with his legs crossed. His arm gestures are expansive.

Legs are crossed

USING TESTS

There are numerous tests available that can be used to estimate a candidate's ability – either their level of intelligence or a specific technical skill. Panel interviews and role-playing are also popular methods of testing the skills of a candidate.

69 Use only tests that have been devised by a reputable source.

POINTS TO REMEMBER

- Tests should not replace face-to-face interviews, but rather they should augment them.
- Personality tests produce a profile of an individual's main characteristics, but they do not tell you whether the candidate is going to be good at the job.
- You can have personality tests tailor-made for your organization or buy them off the shelf.
- With most personality tests, staff need to be specially trained to interpret the results accurately.

PREPARING TO USE TESTS

If you are asking candidates to take any type of test, written or situational, inform them in advance in writing, setting out clearly the criteria by which they will be judged. When deciding which tests to use, choose those that are strictly relevant to the job. Always make sure that they are conducted under the exact conditions stipulated – in some countries legal action can result from a test being improperly conducted. If you intend to hold tests at regular intervals during an employee's time with your organization, that fact should be explained to them at the interview and also be recorded in their job description.

APTITUDE TESTS

These are relatively simple written tests that measure skills, such as reading, writing, verbal reasoning, and numerical ability. They have a built-in "anticheat" factor, which means they produce a very accurate picture of an individual's abilities. If you receive replies from a large number of apparently suitable candidates, invite them to undergo a series of aptitude tests as a time-efficient way to reduce the list. Make sure you have suitable surroundings in which to conduct the tests, since they should be carried out under controlled conditions.

70 Update the tests that you use at regular intervals.

71 Read test results as a whole, not issue by issue.

PERSONALITY TESTS

The term "personality tests" is used generically to cover a variety of verbal, visual, and written tests. They are based on the belief that personal characteristics are measurable and that the presence or absence of certain traits correlates to success in the workplace and thus suitability for a job. To use such testing effectively, you must first establish a clear idea of the job specification and the type of personality that might fit the vacancy.

72 Use psychometric tests to support other tests, rather than on their own.

73 Ask for written applications and ask a graphologist to check them.

PSYCHOMETRIC TESTS

A type of personality test, psychometric tests are widely used to measure the mental ability of candidates under consideration for a job. As an employer, you will probably want to use this method in one of three ways:

- To observe how often a candidate indulges in specific kinds of behavior;
- To discover their powers of self-observation;
- To see how they react in certain set situations.

ANALYZING HANDWRITING

Many major institutions employ graphologists as a matter of course to interpret the characteristics revealed in the handwriting of interviewees. Remember to consider the results of such a test alongside your assessment of a candidate made during an interview, not in isolation.

Regular rhythm of letters indicates consistency

Upward angled t-bars reveal enthusiasm

Starting strokes suggests dependence

Loops in letters show diplomacy

ANALYZING WRITING ▶

When analyzing a candidate's handwriting, do not attempt to make your own subjective judgments – always rely on careful analysis from an expert graphologist.

TECHNICAL TESTS

Consider using panel interviews when recruiting for a vacancy that requires a test of a candidate's specialist knowledge, for example in engineering. Decide beforehand on the areas of questioning that each member of the panel will handle – you could concentrate on the candidate's resume, while your colleagues could ask detailed technical questions. The pressure in this kind of interview is unrelenting and often exposes lack of experience.

Technical expert leads questioning on relevant experience

Lead interviewer finds out about resume

Personnel manager checks up on details

▲ TESTING BY PANEL
If you take on the role of lead interviewer, keep a tight control on the proceedings and do not let anyone present stray from the object of the test – to find out about the interviewee and his or her knowledge.

74 Ask any internal candidates why they want to move.

INTELLIGENCE TESTS

The IQ (Intelligence Quotient) test is now mainly used for comparing children of school age. As an employer, you can make use of various more sophisticated means of measuring verbal, abstract, and numerical reasoning, which have been specially prepared for use in the workplace. Great confidence is placed internationally on the GMAT (Graduate Management Admissions Test), which has become a prerequisite for entry into most of the better-quality business schools.

SITUATIONAL TESTS

Putting candidates into a simulated work situation allows you to judge how they might perform on the job. Carry out situational testing in the final stages of the interviewing process, by which time you will have reduced the number of candidates to a shortlist. However, even if the test is very realistic, it will never simulate relationships between individual colleagues that take time to develop and are crucial to personal motivation.

> **75** Remember to warn candidates if you are going to test them.

CHOOSING THE APPROPRIATE TEST FOR AN INTERVIEW

TYPE OF TEST	FACTORS TO CONSIDER
APTITUDE Measures general abilities, such as numerical, written, verbal, and reasoning skills.	● This is useful at the very beginning of the selection and interview process. ● This needs to be conducted in a controlled environment, such as a quiet meeting room.
PERSONALITY Measures personality traits. Psychometric tests are often used for this purpose.	● This is appropriate for sensitive jobs such as in the diplomatic service or a customer-complaints department. ● This test is time-consuming and needs to be carried out in a controlled environment.
HANDWRITING Evaluates aspects of personality using characteristics of handwriting (graphology).	● This is useful only in conjunction with other tests as a way of confirming findings from elsewhere. ● Because handwriting may vary in stressful circumstances, several examples need to be taken.
TECHNICAL Tests for technical abilities for jobs, such as machine operation, that require specific skills.	● This is useful at a later stage in the interview process. ● It may be time-consuming and potentially patronizing to those candidates who are able and experienced with all the relevant qualifications.
INTELLIGENCE Compares a young graduate's score to the average score for people of a similar age.	● This may not be appropriate unless some of the interviewees are recent graduates. ● This is helpful where companies are filtering a lot of similarly qualified young applicants for general training.
SITUATIONAL Places candidates in a work situation relevant to the job for which they have applied.	● This is most meaningful for jobs where working relationships are not a top priority. ● It is not useful for initial selection but is appropriate at later stages in the interviewing process.

CLOSING AN INTERVIEW

*A*ll interviews should be brought to a polite but unhurried conclusion – even if you believe a candidate to be unsuitable. As an ambassador for your company, the way in which you wrap up the interview will create a lasting impression on the candidate.

76 Tell candidates how many other interviews you have scheduled.

77 Keep an open mind throughout an interview.

78 Give candidates a chance to withdraw their applications.

INVITING QUESTIONS

Toward the end of an interview, ask the candidates if they have any questions. If they have taken the trouble to find information about your organization, they will have at least one interesting question.

Most questions, however, arise spontaneously from issues discussed in the interview. These are often about specific details of the job and its prospects. Take time when preparing to ensure you can answer most of the reasonable questions that may come up. You can learn much about candidates from how they put questions: for example, those who start with phrases such as "I know this is a silly question, but…" may be prone to undermining their own value and are unlikely to present a confident image of your company.

ENCOURAGING QUESTIONS

If a candidate is stumped for questions to ask, and you do not think he is suitable for the job, thank him and close the interview. Otherwise, summarize the points covered in the interview to see if that stimulates a question, or suggest a line of questioning:

Is there anything more I can tell you about the structure of the department?

You seemed concerned about the training involved. Do you want to ask me about that?

Are there any aspects of the job that you are not clear on and would like clarifying?

TYING UP LOOSE ENDS

At the end of an interview, check that you have found out all you need to know about a candidate. Find out how much notice they need to give in order to leave their present job. Let them know when you will contact them if you want them to attend a second interview, and whether this is likely to be by phone or in writing. Tell them, if appropriate, to contact you if they have not heard from you by the specified time. Above all, consider candidates' feelings: be honest and explicit in any instructions or information that you give them.

Handshake is firm and courteous

Interviewer thanks candidate for attending

◀ THANKING A CANDIDATE
Stand up to signal the end of an interview, thank the candidate for coming to see you, and shake hands. It is polite to do this even if you know they are not suitable for the job.

79 Always preserve the dignity and self-esteem of a candidate.

MAKING A SPONTANEOUS OFFER

You may decide at the end of an interview that you have just met the ideal candidate for the job. Do not risk losing them – ask them immediately if they are genuinely interested in the vacancy, and if they say yes, make them a provisional offer. Although this is not common practice in many businesses, it is often prudent to follow your instincts in certain situations. Make sure, however, that your decision is a rational one and that you have not been carried away by the moment.

ANALYZING AN INTERVIEW

Once the interview is over, assess the information you
have gathered. Use this, along with a second interview,
to help make your final selection.

RECORDING IMPRESSIONS

*A*fter *conducting several interviews, they
may all begin to blur into each other.
Make memory-jogging notes as soon as
a candidate has left the room so that you
will be able to distinguish the characteristics
of one applicant from those of another.*

80 If you are in
doubt about an
interviewee, trust
your instincts.

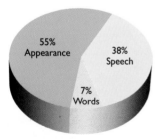

55%
Appearance

38%
Speech

7%
Words

▲ **FIRST IMPRESSIONS**
*About 55 percent of our first impressions of
a person are formed by their appearance,
38 percent by the way they speak, and
a mere 7 percent by the words they use.*

NOTING YOUR INSTINCTS

Instincts are a powerful and useful tool and
should not be ignored. They are backed by years
of subconsciously extracting and compiling
information from experience and provide valid
pointers to individual characters. Always note
your first impressions of every candidate, because
at that point your instincts will be working
overtime. Although first impressions rely heavily
on a candidate's appearance and manner, ask
yourself whether you have retained other strong
impressions about them. Were you impressed by
their posture, or did they have an air of confidence?

AVOIDING BIAS

81 Avoid making biased judgments on any of the candidates.

When analyzing an interview, do not allow your personal prejudices to influence you into making judgments about people based on your notions of class, sex, religion, or race. For example, avoid assuming that someone who went to the same college as you is superior to someone who did not. In addition, beware of a built-in bias in any tests you set the candidates; many have been devised using a single social group as a control.

ASKING OTHER OPINIONS

It is always valuable to get a second opinion. For example, if one of your colleagues has previously interviewed a candidate, share your impressions with the other interviewer as soon as possible, and discuss any areas of disagreement. If you are the sole interviewer, however, it is advisable to ask workmates who may have briefly met the candidate for their impressions. Also ask your reception staff how they found a candidate: were they polite, calm, flustered, or nervous? Add their impressions to your own to build up a more complete picture of the individual.

82 Try to imagine what a candidate is like outside the interview room.

ASKING A ▶ RECEPTIONIST
Check with your reception staff to find out what impression a candidate made on them. Their opinion will add extra useful information to your picture of an individual's personality and suitability for the job.

MAKING A SHORTLIST

Once you have recorded your impressions of each candidate, draw up a shortlist of people for a second interview. Ideally, the shortlist should contain the names of between three and six people that you would like to consider further for the job.

83 Inform candidates before carrying out background checks on them.

CHECKING YOUR NOTES

Read through all your notes again – both those that you took during the interview and the impressions and recollections that you jotted down after the candidate had left. Use different colored markers to underline comments about aspects of the candidate's skills and personality. For example, use blue for computer skills, green for relevant experience, and red for personality traits. This will give you an overall impression of each candidate's strengths and weaknesses. Rate all the candidates in this manner, and select the leading ones for further consideration.

84 Keep candidates' resumes with your notes, references, and matching sheets.

EVALUATING CANDIDATES

Now you need to evaluate the candidates against your ideal candidate. To do this, take a blank matching sheet and divide your criteria into those that the candidate must have and those that would be a welcome bonus. Then use the matching sheets that you have prepared for each candidate in order to see which candidates possess the "must-have" qualities. Eliminate the rest. Look through the remaining list and see how many of the "bonus" qualities each candidate possesses. Weight these (optional) qualities according to their importance for the vacancy, and come up with a ranking of the most suitable candidates.

85 Make a separate file for each of the candidates.

86 Do not draw up your shortlist until all candidates have been interviewed.

CHOOSING A SHORTLIST

Check notes on work experience from interview.

▼

Recap on resume and matching sheet.

▼

Confer and seek advice from colleagues.

▼

Consider who best suits your company culture.

▼

Establish a shortlist to interview again.

SHORTLISTING THE CANDIDATES

When you have ranked all the suitable candidates, create the shortlist by selecting the top five or six. Keep the shortlist short – it should consist only of those candidates whom you are going to call for a second interview; lengthening it wastes time and resources. Use the shortlist, along with a brief summary of each candidate's main relevant qualities, to show to any other interviewers or senior management, or put it on file after selection for reference when further recruits are needed.

Decide whether to check candidate references at this point or after the second interview. This may be a long process, but is worth doing early – it is very annoying to settle on your final choice only to find that they have a poor track record. Always ask the candidates before you contact their references; some may be current employers, and contact could compromise the candidate's job.

87 Never compromise requirements if nobody is suitable.

READVERTISING AND ALTERING STANDARDS

If none of the applicants are suitable for a job, you have two options. One is to advertise again – perhaps in a different place – in the hope that you attract better candidates. Alternatively, you can alter the specifications of the job – for example, by allocating some aspects to someone else – and then look for someone qualified for this modified job.

POINTS TO REMEMBER

- There is no perfect candidate.
- If the job has a security aspect (for example, working in a bank) it is worth checking candidate references early.
- One aspect of a candidate's personality should not be allowed to carry too much weight.
- Detailed notes from the interview will ease the shortlisting process.

CALLING SUBSEQUENT INTERVIEWS

When inviting candidates for a second interview, there is little point in taking them through the same procedures and questions as on their first visit. Before you can design a different interview for them, however, decide what you want to get out of it.

88 Offer to pay candidates' travel expenses for their second interviews.

ASSESSING YOUR PURPOSE

You may wish to recall candidates to a second interview for the following reasons:
- To introduce them to other members of the organization;
- To ask them more questions and become better acquainted with them;
- To compare them once again with other shortlisted candidates to determine a "winner";
- To put them through a different set of tests.

89 Ask if candidates still want the job before asking to meet them again.

RECALLING CANDIDATES

When you phone candidates to ask them back for another interview, make sure that they are still interested in the position. Remember to be discreet when you recall them and be sensitive to what is potentially an awkward situation at their current workplace. Organizing interview times may be more difficult the second time around because you will probably need to involve more people – either other people in the hiring process, or colleagues, or top management. In addition, you may also want to arrange the interview times close together so it is easy to compare the remaining candidates while they are fresh in your mind.

▲ **BEHAVING DISCREETLY**
When calling candidates to invite them for a further interview, always make sure that they are able to talk freely.

DECIDING WHICH AREAS TO INVESTIGATE FURTHER

Although there may be specific areas that you feel were insufficiently covered in the first interview, you should use the second interview for testing the candidate against the others on the shortlist. Delve more deeply into each individual's strengths and weaknesses, then compare them with those of the others. It can be appropriate here to look at a candidate's future plans and ambitions. How suitable would he or she be for promotion?

If you are selecting others to assist you in the interview, choose colleagues who can offer specific skills. A director, for example, will have extensive experience in assessing an applicant's potential overall contribution to the company.

90 Set up a filing system to retain the resumes of all the candidates.

91 Decide which questions each of you will ask during the interview.

CHOOSING INTERVIEWERS FOR THE SECOND ROUND

INTERVIEWERS	FACTORS TO CONSIDER
COLLEAGUE A potentially close coworker of the person to be selected.	● Colleagues understand exactly what is involved in the job and therefore which particular candidate is likely to possess the skills best suited for it. ● Colleagues may need to work closely with the candidate; they should find out whether they are going to get along together.
PERSONNEL MANAGER A specialist in human resources.	● The personnel department tends to have the most skilled interviewers in the organization. ● The personnel department can be objective and systematic about the selection process because it is responsible for processing gains and losses of human resources within the organization.
DIRECTOR Experienced in assessment of potential new recruits.	● The presence of a director flatters a new recruit by showing that the appointment is being considered at boardroom level. ● A member of the board can bring to bear his or her wide experience and understanding of the organization's interests.

MATCHING AN APPLICANT TO A JOB

A subsequent interview may be your last chance to decide which candidate is right for the position. It is important to get the most out of all interviews so that you can compare candidates. Consider conducting a test using a real task to check their skills.

92 Remember that personal references often tend to be rather subjective.

93 Ask candidates for the best time to contact references.

HOLDING SUBSEQUENT INTERVIEWS

Remember that you are looking for someone to be effective in a specific job. It is important that you match the abilities of the candidate to the requirements of the job. If you decide to test interviewees, consider carefully which aspects of the job to test them on, and try to make the test as close to a real work task as possible.

TESTING A ▼ CANDIDATE
Use subsequent interviews to test candidates in a specific work-related area.

Interviewee demonstrates his computer literacy

Interviewer supervises a computer test that she has composed

EVALUATING CANDIDATES' SKILLS

Put the job's top 10 requirements in order from the most to the least important.

↓

Give the requirements scores from 10 down to 1.

↓

Grade the candidate's skills on a scale of 10 to 1.

↓

Add together the two grades for each requirement.

↓

Add up the total scores for each candidate.

↓

The two with the the highest scores will be your first and second choices.

95 Do not let one good quality cancel out serious flaws.

94 Ask candidates to explain any discrepancies between what they have told you and their references.

CHECKING REFERENCES

If you are checking a candidate's references at this stage, prepare a list of questions to ask the references – for example, questions about the candidate's time-keeping and their ability to meet deadlines. First, follow up on work-related references, and make sure they are recent. Check how long the reference has known the applicant, and in what capacity. Follow up written references with verbal ones to discuss the applicant's strengths and weaknesses in greater detail. Check with the references on the candidate's interests outside work. What does the declared "charity work" actually involve? Is it a real commitment? How much time does it take up?

MAKING YOUR CHOICE

To select the best applicant for the job, use the chart on the left to make a first and second (backup) choice based on work skills. Compare the candidates' scoring on the job's requirements with your own personal and intuitive feelings about them. This will depend in part on whether you were given satisfactory responses in any areas that you felt needed more questioning. If colleagues were involved in this round of interviews, ask for their opinions and add them to your own. Your final choices should balance technical and personal qualities in the candidates. If you do not have total authority to make the final selection, present your first and second choices to the appropriate manager, then obtain his or her approval of your choice.

MAKING A FINAL OFFER

Howevever pleased and relieved you feel at having found an ideal recruit for your vacancy, spend time attending to the details of the offer. Make the offer verbally, then follow up formally in writing requesting written confirmation of acceptance.

96 Talk through the details of the job offer with your new recruit.

97 Make sure your salaries are fair and competitive.

98 To avoid confusion, confirm a job offer in writing.

OFFERING A JOB VERBALLY

Begin by offering a job verbally – either on the spot at the end of the second interview or by phone. Outline the benefits package that comes with the position, and allow the candidate time to ask questions. If your verbal offer is rejected, ask if this is negotiable. If the reply is still a refusal, turn your attention to your second choice. In some cases, your chosen candidate may go back to their current employer and ask them to match your offer; in such a case you need to decide if you are willing to negotiate further with the applicant.

CONFIRMING IN WRITING

If your verbal offer is accepted, follow it up as soon as possible with written confirmation of the terms and conditions of the job. An agreement is not binding until a written offer has been accepted in writing. If you are in charge of drafting an offer letter, make sure that it includes:

● Job title, description, and working hours;
● Annual salary;
● The company benefits package;
● Any conditions that the offer is subject to, such as the completion of a medical examination;
● A date by which the prospective employee must sign and return the written job offer to accept the terms and conditions of the job.

HANDLING COUNTEROFFERS

People with skills that are in demand (in financial markets, for example) may play your offer against an offer from their present (or another) company to improve their salary. If you decide to increase your offer in response to this, establish that you will not consider doing so again, and set a deadline for a final acceptance or rejection.

NEGOTIATING A SALARY

Salary negotiations should always be left as late as possible in the interview process. Your priority is to get the best possible candidate at the lowest possible price – in that order. Prepare a strategy for presenting a salary offer, then decide how to bargain if the candidate rejects it. Check that the salary you are offering is comparable to the rest of your field. If not, modify the salary so that it is competitive, but keep the company budget in mind while doing so. Look at other ways of making the package more attractive. Can you offer more benefits instead of more money, such as a company car or complete dental care? Can you offer a salary review after a short period of employment or a non-contributory pension plan? Is there a performance-related bonus plan that the candidate can quickly become part of?

HANDLING THE RESPONSE TO YOUR LETTER

Having sent your offer letter, expect to hear from your chosen candidate within the time limit you set. In most instances, anticipate a positive reply and proceed with organizing a starting date. If, however, you receive a written rejection to your offer, turn again to your previous shortlist. Deal on an individual basis with candidates who respond with further demands; these may be negotiable. For example, if you regard a request for a higher salary instead of a company car to be acceptable, both you and your new recruit will benefit.

Short and concise letter arrives promptly

▼ **WRITING QUICKLY**
A new recruit will be unwilling to resign from their present job until you send the written offer letter. Do this quickly so that they can complete their notice period and begin the new job at the earliest opportunity.

99 Give the candidate a date by which to reply to your offer.

DEALING WITH UNSUCCESSFUL APPLICANTS

Always notify unsuccessful applicants as soon as possible, especially if they have been shortlisted. If they are curious to know why they have been rejected, it is helpful to give them constructive feedback that might assist them in their future job searches.

100 Imagine yourself to be the recipient when writing a rejection letter.

POINTS TO REMEMBER

● Business environments change, and yesterday's reject may be tomorrow's hot property.

● Rejected candidates may be suitable to fill vacancies elsewhere in the organization.

● A rejected candidate should be informed if you intend to pass his or her details on to another person or department.

● An applicant's details are confidential even after they have been rejected.

● Everyone is rejected at some time in their lives, but you should be as kind and positive as possible when breaking news of a rejection.

◄ WRITING A REJECTION LETTER
Failure to send a polite reply as quickly as possible to unsuccessful candidates creates the impression of an ill-mannered and badly managed organization.

REJECTING IN WRITING

It is a matter of courtesy to write to every rejected candidate, letting them know of your decision. Be polite and succinct, thanking each candidate for their interest in the post, and explaining, in general terms, why they were unsuccessful in the application. At this late stage in the recruitment process, the numbers of candidates concerned will not be vast, so try to write individual letters.

Dear Ms. Dartford

Thank you for attending the interview on January 18th for the position of overseas sales manager with TRC.

I regret that in this instance we are unable to offer you the job. We had a very strong response to our advertisement, with a number of first-class applicants for the position, including yourself. While we appreciate your linguistic skills, we feel that your lack of detailed technical knowledge of engineering would be a drawback.

With your permission, we will keep your details on our files for future reference.

Yours sincerely
Doris Fisher
Manager, Human Resources

Thank candidates for attending interviews

Be straightforward in your wording of rejection

Give a valid reason for rejection

Ask if you can keep candidate details on file

KEEPING DETAILS ON FILE

After checking that they are agreeable, keep the details of all relevant job applicants on file. If you have already started a database of such applicants, update it in the light of your interviews. If appropriate, make your colleagues aware of any particularly promising candidates that you have rejected for a post – this may be a cost-effective way of filling another vacancy, since it cuts down on further advertising costs.

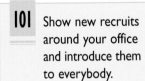

101 Show new recruits around your office and introduce them to everybody.

CULTURAL DIFFERENCES

It is common practice in North America to reject unsuccessful applicants in a fairly blunt and straightforward manner, since failure is considered a step to success. In Japan, however, the tone and phrasing of a rejection is very subtle to avoid offending the disappointed candidate.

RESPONDING TO QUERIES

If you receive calls from rejected candidates who would like to know why you have turned them down, always give a reason. Do not be evasive or put them off by saying you will call them back. Deal with them honestly, there and then, since any information and advice that you can give about their performance may be of use to them in their next interview. If the first impression you had of someone was that they looked unkempt, pass that message on, but couch it in polite terms: "Your appearance could benefit from a little attention," is less offensive than "You were a mess."

LETTING DOWN REJECTED CANDIDATES LIGHTLY

Always be polite and constructive when rejecting candidates, either verbally or by letter. Introduce a reassuring phrase or two to soften the blow, but never make feeble excuses.

 Your lack of proficiency in German is a drawback, since we expect Germany to become an important market.

 We feel that the job needs more line-management experience than you are yet able to bring to it.

 You have considerable talents; we would like to keep in touch in case something else comes up.

 We have offered the job to a person with a perfect match of skills. You were the next contender.

ASSESSING YOUR ABILITY

Practice is the most productive way of developing and improving your interviewing technique. Chart your progress and performance as an interviewer by responding to the following statements, then mark the options closest to your experience. Be as honest as you can: if your answer is "never," mark Option 1; if it is "always," mark Option 4; and so on. Add your scores together, then refer to the Analysis to see how you scored. Use your answers to identify the areas that need most improvement.

OPTIONS
1 Never
2 Occasionally
3 Frequently
4 Always

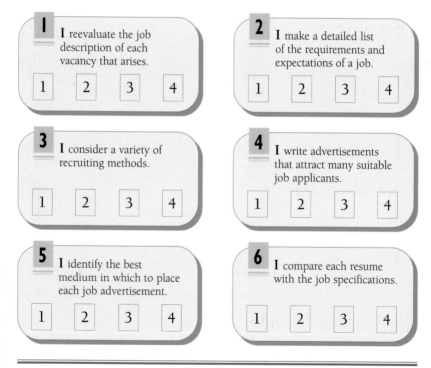

1 I reevaluate the job description of each vacancy that arises.

1   2   3   4

2 I make a detailed list of the requirements and expectations of a job.

1   2   3   4

3 I consider a variety of recruiting methods.

1   2   3   4

4 I write advertisements that attract many suitable job applicants.

1   2   3   4

5 I identify the best medium in which to place each job advertisement.

1   2   3   4

6 I compare each resume with the job specifications.

1   2   3   4

7 I choose a suitable location in which to conduct interviews.

1   2   3   4

8 I prepare myself thoroughly before any interviews take place.

1   2   3   4

9 I brief colleagues clearly before panel interviews.

1   2   3   4

10 I review a candidate's resume and letter just before an interview.

1   2   3   4

11 I know how to make a flustered or nervous candidate feel relaxed.

1   2   3   4

12 I control the course of an interview confidently.

1   2   3   4

13 I take care to verify a candidate's claimed qualifications.

1   2   3   4

14 I ask each candidate to account for any gaps in their employment history.

1   2   3   4

15 I encourage each candidate to talk about their previous experience.

1   2   3   4

16 I encourage timid candidates to speak about themselves with confidence.

1   2   3   4

17 I examine each candidate's strengths and weaknesses.

1   2   3   4

18 I give each candidate a clear, positive picture of the organization.

1   2   3   4

19 I ask candidates how they feel they can benefit our organization.

1   2   3   4

20 I spend the majority of an interview listening to what a candidate is saying.

1   2   3   4

21 I am objective about what a candidate is saying throughout an interview.

1   2   3   4

22 I am polite to each candidate and show interest in their points of view.

1   2   3   4

23 I assess whether a candidate will fit in with the organization.

1   2   3   4

24 I conduct tests, if necessary, to establish that a candidate can do the job.

1   2   3   4

25 I gain additional insights by watching and reading a candidate's body language.

1   2   3   4

26 I remain attentive and interested throughout each interview.

1   2   3   4

27 I note down my first impressions immediately after each interview.

1   2   3   4

28 I ask for a second opinion on all shortlisted candidates.

1   2   3   4

29 I establish how soon a candidate can join the organization.

1   2   3   4

30 I conduct negotiations over the salary and benefits package smoothly.

1   2   3   4

31 I send rejection letters promptly to all unsuccessful applicants.

1   2   3   4

32 I ensure confidentiality at all times.

1   2   3   4

ANALYSIS

Now that you have completed the self-assessment, add up your total score and check your performance by reading the corresponding evaluation. Whatever level of success you have achieved during the interviews, it is important to remember that there is always room for improvement. Identify your weakest areas, then refer to the sections in this book where you will find practical advice and tips to help you establish and hone your interviewing skills.

32–64: Your skills need improving. Learn from your mistakes and take time to prepare well for every interview that you hold.
65–95: Your interviewing skills are fairly sound, but certain areas still need improvement.
96–128: You have a successful interviewing technique. Continue to look for ways to develop your interviewing style.

INDEX

ACKNOWLEDGMENTS

AUTHOR'S ACKNOWLEDGMENTS

The production of this book has called on the skills of many people. I would like particularly to mention my editors at Dorling Kindersley, and my assistant Jane Williams.

PUBLISHER'S ACKNOWLEDGMENTS

Dorling Kindersley would like to thank Emma Lawson for her valuable part in the planning and development of this series, everyone who generously lent props for the photoshoots, and the following for their help and participation:

Editorial Tracey Beresford, Anna Cheifetz, Michael Downey, Jane Garton, Adèle Hayward, Catherine Rubinstein, David Tombesi-Walton; **Design** Helen Benfield, Darren Hill, Ian Midson, Simon J. M. Oon, Kate Poole, Nicola Webb, Ellen Woodward; **DTP assistance** Rachel Symons; **Consultants** Josephine Bryan, Jane Lyle; **Indexer** Hilary Bird; **Proofreader** David Perry; **Photography** Steve Gorton; **Additional photography** Andy Crawford, Tim Ridley; **Photographers' assistants** Sarah Ashun, Nick Goodall, Lee Walsh; **Illustrators** Joanna Cameron, Yahya El-Droubie, Richard Tibbetts.

Models Angela Cameron, Kuo Kang Chen, Patrick Dobbs, Carole Evans, Vosjava Fahkro, John Gillard, Ben Glickman, Zahid Malik, Sotiris Melioumis, Mutsumi Niwa, Ted Nixon, Mary-Jane Robinson, Kiran Shah, Lois Sharland, Tessa Woodward; **Make-up** Elizabeth Burrage, Lynne Maningley.

Special thanks to the following for their help throughout the series:
Ron and Chris at Clark Davis & Co. Ltd for stationery and furniture supplies; Pam Bennett and the staff at Jones Bootmakers, Covent Garden, for the loan of footwear; Alan Pfaff and the staff at Moss Bros, Covent Garden, for the loan of the men's suits; David Bailey for his help and time; Graham Preston and the staff at Staverton for their time and space; and Anna Youle for all her support and assistance.

Suppliers Austin Reed, Church & Co., Compaq, David Clulow Opticians, Elonex, Escada, Filofax, Mucci Bags.

Picture researcher Mariana Sonnenberg; **Picture library assistant** Sam Ward.

PICTURE CREDITS

Key: *b* bottom, *c* center, *l* left, *r* right, *t* top
Tony Stone Images jacket front cover *tr*, 4–5, 39*br*.

AUTHOR'S BIOGRAPHY

Tim Hindle is founder of the London-based business language consulting firm, Working Words, which helps international companies to compose material in English and communicate their messages clearly to their intended audiences. A regular business writer, Tim Hindle has been a contributor to *The Economist* since 1979 and was editor of *EuroBusiness* from 1994 to 1996. As editorial consultant and author, he has produced a number of titles including *Pocket Manager*, *Pocket MBA*, and *Pocket Finance*, and a biography of Asil Nadir, *The Sultan of Berkeley Square*.